Hunting & Fishing

Tips THE PROS CAN'T TELL YOU!!!

TIM ABEL

ILLUSTRATED BY STEVE ROSE

Order this book online at www.trafford.com
or email orders@trafford.com

Most Trafford titles are also available at major online book retailers.

Note for Librarians: A cataloguing record for this book is available from Library
and Archives Canada at www.collectionscanada.ca/amicus/index-e.html

Printed in Victoria, BC, Canada.

ISBN: 978-1-4251-9194-8 (soft)
ISBN: 978-1-425-19195-5 (hard)
ISBN: 978-1-4251-9196-2 (ebook)

*Our mission is to efficiently provide the world's finest, most comprehensive
book publishing service, enabling every author to experience success.
To find out how to publish your book, your way, and have it available
worldwide, visit us online at www.trafford.com*

Trafford rev. 9/3/2009

 www.trafford.com

North America & international
toll-free: 1 888 232 4444 (USA & Canada)
phone: 250 383 6864 ♦ fax: 812 355 4082

Dedications

This book is dedicated to my wife, Kim. Without her love, support, and evil looks from time to time, I would not have been inspired to capture these thoughts in written form.

This book is also dedicated to Dale Peterson. I may not be alive today if it were not for Dale's help on a bad day on Leech Lake.

Introduction

As an avid hunter and fisherman, I have been glued to every hunting and fishing magazine I could get my hands on over the past several years. I have literally learned most of everything I know about hunting from 15 minute knowledge bursts sitting on the toilet everyday. I started hunting nine years ago at the ripe old age of 35. Thirty five is not old in most communities, but it is rather long in the tooth to be taking up a sport like hunting. It is for this reason that I am uniquely qualified to write this book of tips. Most of the tips we read about are from life long hunters and pros that have put small GPS systems in their deer feed for tracking purposes. They know the exact time that big bucks are to arrive at any particular spot on any given day. In fact, I have heard that some deer have signed contracts just to show up on camera at appointed times. The experts never make mistakes and if they do, they have the uncanny ability to make you believe that everything played out the way they planned. As captivating as some of the shows and articles are to watch and read they are of little help to those of us that have never seen anything larger than small 8 or 10 pointers wishing to commit suicide while slowly grazing. I have never harvested a B&C or a P&Y Buck. I have taken the largest buck off our hunting property in over 20 years, but I know that I was just in the right place at the right time. I believe my buck even left a suicide note.

By no means do I desire to belittle great hunter's talents, but O'Neill Williams, Jackie Bushman, Ted Nugent, along with writers like Bill Heavey and Patrick McManus and so many more have far too much class to go where I am going to go in this book. They have too much at stake to share too much stupidity with the world.

I write from a man's perspective because that is all I know. For all you outdoors women that may be reading this book, please understand that I respect you, but I am just too lazy to write him/her throughout the entire book. I have no clue as to the difficulty women go through just to stay scent free; furthermore, the burden women must go through just to relieve their bladders while balancing in a tree stand must equate to a redneck version of Chinese Circus acrobatics. I would welcome reading a similar book written from a woman's perspective.

If it were not for all my hunting friends like Mike Simonds and Mike McClain, I would just be sitting in the woods during hunting season. I doubt you could categorize what I did in the woods my first few years as hunting. Jack Holcomb and Kenny Dunn run the Riverdale Gun Club and do their best to insure everyone is safe and happy. It is a difficult job keeping 16 hunters happy, but they do a great job. I am blessed to be in a club with 15 lifelong hunters that were all born in the woods. Some can call owls over their head. Others don't need a grunt tube. Don't ask me which end they blow out to call the deer, but it is beyond me how they do it. Still others just have the ability to disappear in the woods just beyond the tree line only to reappear with blood stained hands needing some help dragging their buck(s) out of the woods. It is these same friends that helped me by telling me half of everything I needed to know before I went into the woods. The other half of that information is encapsulated in this book of tips. You can always rely on a friend to tell you the other half of what you need to know when the hunting day is over.

Fishing is something that I have been doing all my life, but I only started bass fishing 20 years ago and I have never Fly fished. To that end, there are many of you that will say, "Tim, you have not fished enough to write a book of tips". In most cases I would agree, but not this one. Some fishermen, like me, can find new and exciting ways to screw up anything from using the right bait incorrectly to improperly casting in tight quarters. All the tips provided have been proven and I can give at least one example of why to take any of these tips to heart. I have the scares and a hunched back stuffed with excessive amounts of humility to prove it.

This tips book could not be complete without a chapter on hunting and fishing tips for the home front. Would you agree that a big part of every hunting and fishing trip begins with making things right at home so you can go without worry? A major rule of thumb here is that "If Mamma ain't happy, nobody is happy". Do you want to enjoy hunting without worrying if your wife is pissed? I can't help you? Nobody can, that feeling will remain with you your entire life in the woods. Want to avoid the "Manson Lamps" when you walk in the door each weekend? Are you less concerned about coyotes than your wife's eyes gleaning through you with a squint that says, "You had your fun and your mine now, all mine"? I might be able to help a little. My wife has a look that will shoot right though me and I have to think and act quickly to please her. I need to kill something with 6+ legs smaller than a corn seed, punish one or both of the kids, or just sit down with her and watch a movie on the Life/Death-Time for Women or the WE-Estrous channel. My wife would rather watch Susan Sarandon die over the longest 2 hour movie ever recorded than see John Wayne take a bullet to the heart at the very end of The Sands of Iwo Jima (Sorry if I have blown the ending for the 2 or 3 of you who have not seen this movie). John Wayne is immortal in our house and as far as my wife is concerned John Wayne and Elvis should never die, even in a movie. Men can handle other men dying and getting blown up in movies, but no harm should ever come to a woman or child in anything called entertainment as far as I am concerned. So we compromise, but enough already.

Wives do not care why you are late. They don't care that you had to track the deer you shot 2 miles up hill in the rain. They don't care if your outboard engine fell off in the middle of the lake. You were not around that day when she needed to talk, vent, glare, clean up after the dog, or when the spider crawled over her toes. On the other end of the spectrum, all that is going through your mind when you walk in the door from hunting and fishing is "how and when should I bring up hunting or fishing next weekend". You will find a few tips that might make life a little better in those situations, but those "Manson Lamps" are only 50%

treatable. Any slip up here can postpone hunting and fishing for weeks at a time.

The recipe section of the book is included because I am not a chef, but I have some great tips for using Dales Steak sauce and Worcestershire sauce. Any chef would cringe at this, but the results are incredible and too easy not to share. These are not "My" recipes, but I have a few unique twists. The results have turned vegetarians into venison jerky and backstrap craving lunatics.

To summarize, these tips and stories could help you get on a buck. They could help you get on a big fish. They may help your home life as well. Most importantly, I hope you get a good laugh at the mistakes I have made over the years. Happy hunting and fishing!

Contents

Chapter I

Hunting Tips

Don't check the wind by licking your finger an hour or so after spreading deer urine. There is not enough Gatorade in the world to get that taste out of your mouth. If this happens to you, leave the woods immediately for the Waffle House.

Don't be seen taking an empty plastic soda bottle into the woods as a pee bottle. "Real Men" use Gatorade bottles with a wider top. Bigger targets are better, unless you use your own pee as an attractant. Remember to take the wrapper off to make it a little quieter in the woods.

Never trust an old wooden tree stand, advice from a competitive hunter, or a fart in the deer stand. All three stink far more than anticipated.

If you are out of shape when hunting season starts, or if you know you just smell bad to a deer, bring your scent free deodorant with you to your tree stand. Use it on your forehead and neck after you stop the initial floodgates of perspiration. Your hunt will be much dryer and scent free, quickly.

Abel's Waffle House Theory – The Waffle House is the greatest restaurant in the world after any hunting or fishing trip. The reverse is true before any hunting and fishing trip.

Drop a bullet on your deer stand. Tap your wedding ring loudly against your tree stand. Drop your water bottle. Do something wrong and make at least one mistake getting set up for your hunt. I have never taken a deer without making a mistake. The deer know if you are on your game and will not come out, unless they think you are not a very good hunter.

Good deer stand placement will make up for some of your lack of hunting skills. Place your stand a little deeper in the woods from any tree line than other experienced hunters might. I believe deer can spot a novice blink an eye. Face north, near the top of a hill if possible to take advantage of the wind coming out of the north on the cold days. This will also provide better action for hunters with scent control problems such as smoking and residual side effects from the "Scattered, Smothered, Covered, and Chunked" hash browns you had earlier in the day.

Don't pinch your nose to stop a sneeze when a big buck walks up one you after eating eggs, bacon, sausage or hash browns unless you are wearing scent free Depends.

Wash your hunting boots in no scent detergent a couple weeks before hunting season starts. Remember the deer you took in December? Did use your boots on one or more work days at the hunting property? You may not smell it, but your boots stink!!!

Don't Bust Your Head Open!!!

A. Be careful with shots to your left if you are right handed and to the right if you are left handed when using high powered rifles. Insure you have at least five fingers of eye relief between your eye and the scope or you will bust your head open with the recoil.

B. Replace your scope the "First" time you cut your head open between the eyes. Don't assume you are the problem.

C. When bleeding like a stuck pig from the forehead and nose, bleed on your hunting cloths, not your deer stand or the ground. You can change your clothes later.

It is worse to cut your head open with your scope while killing a deer than it is to shoot and miss a deer. The scar between your eyes will be noticed every day, week, and year at the hunting camp. You only catch grief about missing until the next sucker misses.

Use your t-shirt or camo t-shirt as TP if you forget to bring any TP in the woods. T-shirts are a couple dollars and camo t-shirt are $5 at Wal-Mart near the end of every hunting season. You must ask yourself at the time, "Is it worth $5 not to use leaves". (The side tip here is to avoid Chigger bites on the butt at all cost during the rut.)

Use clear nail polish on chigger bites on the butt during hunting season and you won't get busted by a buck while scratching your butt.

Bring a couple washcloths with you in a plastic baggie on the hot days in the woods. I put a couple ice cubes in the bag and wet the cloths with some filtered water. I also spray some of the "No Scent" spray in the baggie. This will make your hunt on hot days much more tolerable. Camo bandanas are better than washcloths, unless you can find camo washcloths.

Don't wear overalls while hunting after eating "Scattered, Smothered, Covered, and Chunked" hash browns. Any remnants of butt nuggets on your straps will be noticeable immediately when you re-clip. Better to avoid the problem all together and lose the overalls before the hunt.

Before you shoot an average sized doe with your bow in the last few minutes of hunting light on opening day of bow season, be sure the guys you are hunting with are into tracking a doe in the dark for 2-3 hours. If not, you are better off only taking does in the morning hunt with a bow.

If you use "No Scent" soap when you shower before your hunt, cut off about 25% of the bar of soap to take to the hunting club with you. It is nice to have on those 90 degree days during bow season. Take a hand towel with you and some bottled water to wash yourself down before the evening hunt.

Never drag the carcass of the deer you just skinned and quartered 40 yards upwind of the president of your hunting club's trailer and leave it. This is especially true your first year in the club. After you are established in the club for a few years, the reverse is true. This is a great prank, if your club president has a great sense of humor. (My guess is he does not!)

Take a drink of water 45 minutes before last light if you have a scratchy throat or if you are a smoker. The presence of a deer and a very dry throat can cause an uncontrolled cough and bye, bye deer.

Always make sure your cell phone is on vibrate when you go in the woods. I always thought that was a no-brainer! (Did you know The Allman Brothers ring tones can be heard for 200 yards or more on a clear day!)

Never assume there is enough room in the pee bottle for a 3rd or 4th pee if you have had more than two cups of coffee. You are better off just peeing off your stand or down the tree instead of peeing all over your clothes, deer stand and scope in a panic.

When you cull a good buck because the rack looks a little strange and your hunting buddies may want it out of the gene pool, be sure it's not the biggest buck your friends have ever seen taken before calling it a culled buck. No matter what the name of the buck was, it will forevermore be called "The Culled Buck".

Don't take pictures of squirrels. If you take a camera into the stand like I do to take some wild life photos, make sure the picture you want to take is worth you getting busted. Owls, deer, coyotes, bear and other wildlife make great photos and keepsakes from the hunt and are worth the risk at times. How do you think I felt all day after getting busted by a buck while taking a picture of a squirrel that morning?

Four times is the charm…

A buddy of mine took three shots at two doe out of one of my stands this year and missed all three. Later that day he shot a trophy eight standing where the does were that he missed in the morning. It does not matter if you shoot out of your stand in the morning. Go ahead and get right back in if you shot your rifle that morning at a doe. A buck may be following that trail 6 - 24 hours later. Everyone can't be an Audie Murphy with a gun, so the fall back skill is always persistence.

Don't run out of your hunting area with a loaded weapon just to pee. This sounds like basic advice, but young hunters want to respect others' hunting areas too much sometimes. Also, if you are a coffee drinker, wear boxers and not briefs for quick access during emergencies.

Don't get in the habit of leaving your safety off because it is loud when clicked off, even if you are hunting on the ground. Besides the obvious safety reasons too numerous to mention, taking the safety off is a key part of the hunting process and is required to pull the trigger. If this sounds like you, let me know when you pull the trigger and miss a shot at a trophy buck because you forgot to take the safety off. Get in the habit of taking the safety off only when your target is in the cross hairs and you may not even need to grunt to stop the deer.

If you ever wanted to know how long it takes to reload a muzzleloader after you drop a deer, it takes about 10 seconds longer than it takes for the wounded deer to get up and run off.

Careful making jokes about PETA members at your wife's parties. Any reference to PETA members tasting like chicken or jerky when filleted right could be misinterpreted as the truth. Remember, most of them are already nuts, don't give them anymore ammunition to go off on you.

Don't run out of the woods with a loaded weapon to take a dump during your hunt, especially if you have eaten at the Waffle House for breakfast. You won't make it anyway! Just drop trow by a tree near your stand and bury the pile. There must be something in the food at the Waffle House. Hunters have taken over 4 deer in the last 4 years from a stand where I had recently buried my breakfast.

Take an old winter hunting glove into the stand with you if you have a cold or if you are a smoker. Cough into the winter glove. This will muffle the sound better than the gadgets sold for that purpose, but using the glove instead will allow you to get more junk out of your throat with just one muffled cough.

Wear a face mask and gloves in the woods while hunting. Just the act of taking any one of these items off seems to attract deer. If you are like me, you should hear a very distinct blowing sound behind you the first time you remove one of these items.

Be very careful breaking off leg bones when processing your deer. Use the saw even if you are sure you remember Steven Seagal's techniques from the movie you watched earlier that week. Leg bones can be sharp as a razor and if your spot of impact is not at lest 3 inches below the saw marks, you could slice you hand open like grapefruit. It is also a good idea to keep a First Aid kit around when processing deer.

If you have not seen a deer for a couple hours on a day with a constant light wind, make a phone call, eat, or smoke if you are a smoker. I took 3 doe this year talking on the phone and one with a cigarette in my mouth. I believe deer are eaves dropping on my calls or they might just like the smell of Marlboro Red's. If you remain a non-smoker, you will take trophy deer. Smoke and you will only take does.

Go further into the woods and keep your orange on when you have to "cop a squat" in December. Remember that a big, bright, white hunter's butt can look like a huge Albino buck's butt by other hunters passing on their 4-wheelers at a bad time. Moreover, you will be doomed to be the butt of several "Deliverance" jokes when you get back to camp, if you are spotted.

Tip the ladies well at your local Waffle House. If you are going to be there every weekend all season long, see if the ladies don't push the new grill-man to get your orders out quickly. Waffle House waitresses have memories like alpha-does that bust you year-in and year-out.

Before going to lunch after a successful morning hunt double check your boots and arms for meat, fat, or blood. Mothers and children out for a Saturday brunch just after watching Bambi can look horrified at the site of venison scraps.

Practice new calls from hunting shows before entering the woods. I heard on a show this past fall that I need to blow harder into my grunt tube. Bucks blow loud and so should I. I did not know that a grunt tube call can sound like a children's party favor at the top of a mountain on a clear fall morning. It will also scare off everything for miles.

Shave with no-scent soap before hunting everyday. I have scared off more than one deer by scraping my 5 o'clock shadow across a fleece coat and it never hurts to use more no-scent soap.

Make a scent bomb by taping a hand warmer to a Tink's scent holder. Coat the wick with scent and chunk it partially opened anywhere you need the scent within 30 yards of your stand. They sound like pinecones falling and you have heated scent around you without stomping around your hunting area and stinking it up.

Woodpeckers!!! – Don't' do it. I believe they are protected, but damn!!! I know you want to just blast one from the tree in front of you, but we have to resist the temptation. I honestly believe they are warning the deer of our whereabouts in some kind of animal Morris code.

Squirrels!!! – Don't do it. I know you are often board and they are pissing you off with every pattern of steps they take through the leaves, but damn!!! I don't know if I can hold out on this one. One day Rocky may have to die!

When hunting with your daughter's underwear model boyfriend, always take the time to string your deer up in a tree and skin and quarter it on the spot. Be sure to use a sharp knife and make long, accurate slices in the skin. I enjoyed the look on his face when I pulled the skin from the tailbone to the neck in one quick motion. You will too!!!

Chapter II

Packing Lists

City boys packing list for the morning hunt in the deer stand

- o Browning "A" Bolt Medallion 7 Mag, 300 Win Mag, or 8" Holitzer will do
- o Extra cushion
- o Extra poncho even on sunny day
- o Extra flashlight
- o Extra bullets beyond those in clip or magazine
- o 1 Gatorade
- o 1 water
- o 2 sandwiches, with Grey Poupon mustard, of course
- o 2 granola bars
- o 1 bag beef jerky
- o 1 roll TP
- o 1 package wet naps or wipies
- o 1 decongestant
- o 2 Tylenol
- o 4 Advil
- o 1 Imodium, Pepto Bismol tablet, or Tums
- o Lip balm
- o Eye drops
- o Nose spray
- o Gas-ex
- o Tux Pads
- o Q-tips
- o Reading material
- o GPS
- o Compass
- o Water proof matches
- o Flint and steel because you got it for Christmas and its real cool to have
- o Blackberry or just bring the I-Phone

- Ear piece
- Sun glasses
- Bug spray
- No scent for after the bug spray
- Smokes
- Extra lighter
- Orange vest and hat
- Binoculars to use if bored reading
- 1 pack Vicks cough drops (Cherry flavored)
- Gum
- Summer gloves
- Winter gloves
- Summer mask
- Winter mask
- Extra doe estrogen for back-up for the one spilled all over your boot by accident
- No Doze or other caffeine pills
- Boot mittens
- Hand warmers
- Toe warmers
- French vanilla coffee in the thermos
- 2 knives – 1 for the deer and one for the fingernails if bored reading and glassing
- Fanny Pack
- Mountable umbrella to the tree in case of Poncho malfunction
- AM / FM radio with ear piece for MP3 and I-Pod Touch
- 1 Power Bar – no need for 2 as this is just a 4-5 hour hunt

Country boys packing list for the morning hunt in the deer stand

- o Grampa's old lever action 30/30 or single shot 30.06
- o Extra bullet for hunting and 10 more for shooting signs on the way back home
- o Small baggie of venison jerky fresh off the dehydrator from last weeks hunt
- o Canteen of water
- o Camo ball cap representing favorite SEC team
- o Nextel push and talk or walkie talkie
- o Knife
- o Orange vest

Chapter III

Vishy-swa and Other Reasons
Not to Call!!!

Vishy-swa and Other Reasons Not to Call!!!

There is just something special about being in a deer stand or in a boat. Be it the anticipation of getting the buck of a lifetime or a 10 pound bass, my nerves begin to calm and all the stress from work and home are gone. After an hour of sitting still in the woods or casting, an outdoorsman gets as close to being "one with nature" as possible without shaving our heads, taking a vow of poverty and moving to Tibet. In the morning sunrise, just seeking a pine breath out oxygen as the frost melts off the southeast side is enough to thwart off all anxiety from the home or office. Seeing an owl swoop down and perch 20 yards from you can make you forget the most daunting of tasks in the mighty "to-do" list. Watching an eagle sore above and pick up a fish will make any day thrilling. As annoying as they are, just seeing a few turkey walk right under you, oblivious to your deer hunting agenda, can wipe away all the mess life brings. (Note that these same turkeys will bust you from 100 yards in turkey hunting season). I could go on endlessly, for some of you, I may already have. The point is that when an outdoorsman is in the woods, it does not take long for him to loose all sense of anything beyond his point of site. All the pressures of the world are gone and I have actually stopped hearing my pulse in my neck a time or two.

Suddenly, during a hunt in late December, my phone started to vibrate. In reaching for my phone, in a failed attempt to prolong my state of being and peace of mind, I hoped this was another hunter with an update or deer sighting. Nope, and I knew better. At that time of night it could only be my wife or mother. All too often they forget and call during the "Red Zone" hours. The "Red Zone" is the first hour of light and the last hour of light, as referred to in our house. It is beyond me to try and define "Dark" in a way that either of them (my wife and mother) will understand. It is difficult because Dark does not really exist. It is just the absence of light. Easy enough to understand, right??!! During what could have been the last hunt of the year for me, I got a call from my mother just as the sun had crested on the horizon signaling all big deer to report to my area. I was deep in the Red Zone. Fearful that something is terribly wrong, I quickly answered. This time she was calling to see if I wanted to come over and pick up some fresh Vishy-swa on the way home. I am so lucky to have such a wonderful mother, but…? Listed below are all the things wrong with this call:

- Mom knows I have gone hunting
- Mom has been told about the Red Zone
- Mom still does not remember that after 43 years I still don't like Vishy-swa
- Vishy-swa is usually served cold, right?
- Should I rush over before it warms?

My wife and mother always get a cheerful whispering reply from me in tense voice when they call because I know they love me, but…!!! I don't hunt anything after dark. The day is over for all deer hunters 30 minutes after sundown. It's more like 20 minutes after sundown for me. I can't see as well anymore and I can't count tines or even see some racks in low light. I have 11 hours to talk about anything in the world they would like to discuss. I'm all ears after dark and I can navigate through the thickest pines while catching up on all I missed. Below are some questions I have asked them to ask themselves before calling at twilight:

- Does he need to come home now?

- If not, is this something that he needs to know now?

- Is this something I, being his wife or mother, need to share with him now?

Assuming that most outdoorsman are hunting or fishing at least 1.5 - 2 hours away from home, there is really never a "yes" answer to any of those questions. Let me give a few extreme examples:

- Sickness and injury - There is someone else that can usually get there within minutes, not hours. There are also nurses available for advice and they are much smarter than any outdoorsman I have ever met.

- Dinner question - Anything warm will do, really, ANYTHING!

- Home Repair - Outdoorsmen stop all home repair when hunting and fishing seasons are at their peaks. Please table the question for weeks or months.

- Bugs – This is why we had a son, to kill bugs and cut the grass. If Joey is not around, I've seen both of these ladies throw shoes with great accuracy. But suggesting this just makes them ornery.

- Shopping or decoration questions - Wow, really! Write it down and send me back to the store to get it rather than calling me from the cashier.

- If said wife or mother is pissed at the outdoorsman for any reason - This is the only good reason to call. Typically the hunter will only be able to whisper a few words. Wives and mothers know this as well. I have a few choice words saved in the back of my head to whisper in just such occasions, but usually fail to recall them when needed.

- Death of a friend or family member - Although this is a touchy subject to address, my wife or mother should ask themselves if the dearly departed would want me to enjoy the entire hunt. Furthermore, if there is a death that has occurred, the deceased is not getting any better. If for some reason the departed will be rising from the dead, I believe I have about 3 days to get there.

- Children in trouble - The anticipation of a beating is worse than the beating. Wives and mother should always wait until well after dark to call any outdoorsman and use the time to instill the "Fear of God" into the kids.

- Just to say I love you - "K", but... really!!!

There is nothing like the first hour of light and the last hour of light when hunting and fishing. We, as outdoorsmen, do all in our power to keep that sun from falling; always loosing, but always longing for one last minute of light. For hunters, the game is over 30 minutes after sundown. On this last hunt, somewhere, all the creatures of the woods were moving. Wives and mothers around the world were up and about seeking reasons to use the phone during that last 30 minutes of light.   Nothing was moving around me during this hunt. I just heard about all the activity from the other hunters. I left for home with a smile knowing that I was loved and that I had some soup to pick up, before warmed.

Chapter IV

The 4-wheeler is there to help, right?

The 4-wheeler is there to help, right?

I have found that the #1 most important tip for all time is to be specific when asking questions, especially if you are new to the game! As an example, when told to go down the dirt road and turn right at the Cats-eye on a tree on the left, a novice hunter might ask how far down the road do I go, how many steps/yards, what is a Cats-eye, where is the cat's-eye (low or high), and anything else he can possibly imagine shy of GPS coordinates.

A cats-eye is a small tack, about the size of a nickel, with florescent paint to help those that need help finding obscure trails and hard to find deer stands. I believe I will begin using Budweiser Neon lights instead. There is no conformation that a Budweiser neon light will scare the deer that I can find on the web. I also know I can find that neon light with the blurriest of vision.

Assuming you found the cats-eye so cleverly stuck near the root of the tree by your hunting buddy, stop and get your bearings before continuing into the woods. This is a great time to dry off and spray some no-scent or rub some dirt and pine on your camos and hands. Keep some clippers handy if you are going through some thick stuff.

You can't see a box stand painted black in a thick pine forest in a new moon phase. It is best to wait until the crack of light to go in, if you aren't completely sure where you are going.

If you try and find your way to black box stand in a thick pine forest while it is still dark, dress down. Take off your coat and gloves. You may want to bring a change of shirt. When you pass the stand and walk another mile to get back to the cats-eye where you began your trek, you will have another dry shirt to wear in on your second try.

When you pass the stand a second time and walk for another mile through the dense forest and work your way back to the cats-eye where you started, it should be about light. Call your friend that gave you these directions in hopes of catching him with a buck walking up to him, and say thanks!

Now that you can see the box stand in the dim light, get settled and hang your coat up where you can and take off the wet clothes and bag them. If you did not bring a bag, just sit quietly and dry off. Think positive thoughts about dumb deer with a poor sense of smell that may not have heard you walking, tripping, and falling for the last 2 hours.

After you shoot the large doe with no sense of smell and poor hearing, it will run 70-100 yards down hill. The deer does not know that you are too exhausted to move. It is instinctive to the deer to go to the most inconvenient place to die. Go locate the deer after about 30 minutes if you hear it crash.

Now, it is time for you to go back and get the 4-wheeler you used to drive up to the main trail about 300 yards away. Although you have never taken a 4-wheeler into the woods to recover a deer, you will be thrilled to know exactly where you are. You will also be comforted by the thought that you have a 4-wheeler and you can take all the time you need.

Getting into the woods to your stand and down to the deer is an easy ride. Getting the deer up on the wheeler and strapped in is another story. You will have to try and pull the deer up, sliding it across the seat, and then roll it over the rack on the back. One, two, or even three bungee cords will not hold the deer in place, unless you have done this before. I had not.

On the way back out with the deer, remember to stop at your stand and get your coat, rifle and fanny pack. Go ahead and put your coat on because it is an easy ride out and you are now good to go, unless you have never worked your way out of the woods with a deer strapped to the back of a 4-wheeler. Then just leave everything there, you'll be back.

Now you are ready to easily navigate through the trees like Tony Stuart dominating Watkins Glenn. It was right about this moment that that I could have used some training on how to use the Reverse button. If you are a novice, as I was at this point, you will probably decide to just man-up on the handle bar with the belief that you can just get off and push yourself out of trouble spots. Remember on the 4th or 5th time you get off the 4-wheeler that you are trying to get a deer out of the woods and there should still be a deer strapped on the back. If not, go back and get the deer and drag it to the new wheeler location, about 50 yards from where you started. Be sure to look for the bungee cords that dropped as you go back for the deer. They can be hard to spot in the pine straw and could have been ground into the mud by a tire.

Repeat this drill another 2-3 times over the next hour and check to see if you are now navigating parallel to the main trail. You may be within 20 yard of the trail, but in enough cover to keep you from seeing the trial. In the future you will not need the cat-eyes anymore because you have now plowed a new big trail of zigzags and loops that will be much easier to find than the small cat-eyes.

Finally, call your friends for help. At this point, the hunt will be over for everyone. You will probably be soaked to the skin at this point from the gallons of perspiration that has secreted from your pores. Also, chances are you are breathing too hard to speak. Call your friends to help and just mutter "help get deer", breath, "not near box-stand", breath, "near cats-eye".

Now you can sit, relax, and pray that you are not having a stroke or a heart attack. Now is also a good time to prepare for the verbal abuse you will receive from the friend that is on his way to help. This will be the friend that will give you the most grief about your lack of any 4-wheeler skills in the woods. Resist popping him in the mouth. You may need him to hold a leg or two when you get back to work gutting, skinning and quartering the deer.

Chapter V

Fishing Tips

Be extra careful docking bass boats at night in the winter. Keep three limbs in contact with the boat at all times and let the driver do most of the work getting you close to the dock. That water gets cold and dark real quick at 2 AM in February.

When trout fishing in waist high water with shorts on, cut the line as soon as you notice that the ten pound trout you have been fighting is actually a gar. There is no lure worth the dance you are about to do with that fish.

Bring a bungee cord with you when you are fishing with a rookie in a canoe or Jon Boat. Use it to tie your tackle box to the canoe. If he tips you over you will save your tackle and have something to beat him with.

Be specific when asking your 8 year old if the plug is in the boat. (Side-tip, check for water coming in your boat immediately upon launching. Don't park the truck until you are sure your boat will be on top of the water when you return.)

When teaching kids to cast and/or fish for bass, try using a finesse worm with little or no weight. With this rig you will minimize the number of flying harpoons. The only hook is embedded in the worm. It is weedless and squeamish little boys and girls can put their own plastic bait on their own hook.

You get great action off of Rattletraps and crank baits using light line. You also get a lure so arrow dynamically designed that a 10 year old can cast it across Lake Michigan, with the right wind. Unless you or anyone attempting to use this bait has very good casting control, don't use this rig around docks and other boats. One of the other great features of the Rattletrap is that hitting a boat off a dock can sound like a hydrogen bomb under water. The advice here is to go with plastic worms, jigs, and flukes, no matter what the pros say, until your casting skills are fine tuned.

While teaching kids to fish for bass, teach them to move the plastic worm with the rod tip only. Then slowly real up the slack while watching the line for a bump or twitch. This is not only a great tactic to slow their retrieve, but it will greatly reduce the number of times that a bass hook could rip through your neck when you are not watching.

Anytime you see someone at a tackle store buying 3 or more packs of any one kind of plastic worm, buy a pack.

Never under any circumstances give your best friend the 1st worm out of a new untried pack. It is amazing how 6-8 pound bass will beat each other up just to get to that worm on your friends first cast.

Casting crank baits 101…

A. Look for hanging branches up to ten feet behind you when casting crank baits from the bank.

B. Wives are not very good at pulling crank baits out of husband's heads. If the skin is passed the barb, you will need more help.

C. Cheer up those waiting at your local emergency room by going to get the lure out of the back of your head. Ask the nurse to call you up to the front several times so that everyone can get a good look and a great laugh at your expense.

The only thing bass hate more than the scent of nicotine is DEET, the active ingredient in most mosquito repellents. We use Bounce fabric softeners but nothing will work as well as the real thing. We choose to get a few more mosquito bites than use anything with DEET. We also choose to get yelled at by the Alpha-female in the house about bird-flu and other tremendous risks that we outdoorsmen take.

If you are fishing on a boat and you feel those hash browns kicking in from your morning breakfast, make sure you "dorp-trow" downwind of friends tied up on the bank waiting for you. They get rather surly if you don't.

Use 8 pound test or less when bass fishing in a canoe with a friend. Setting the hook on a bass using 12-14 pound test will piss off your friend all day long.

Don't tell your fishing buddies that they do not have enough money to get you drunk the night before a windy day on the lake or ocean.

Remember that medium action rods flex more than usual with large crank baits attached. You will only need a few inches of slack, not a foot or more. Did you know that it is actually possible to hook your best friend's new 7' Flipping Stick, with new Shimano reel, on your back swing when using a crank bait! If you hook it well, did you also know that you can cast that 7 foot rod over your head and into the lake? Who da thunk it?

Remember when trying to find your friend's pole that you accidentally cast into the lake in 4-6 feet of water, all you need is a large crank bait on the end of your line to slowly drag the bottom. Save time by not asking your friend to help. He is too busy thinking of ways to hold your feet still while holding you upside down in the water as an alternative solution.

Keep your cell phone in a ziplock baggie on hot days in the woods or when fishing. Perspiration can damage a phone and has killed a couple of mine. Also, fish slime will kill a phone or at least add a distinctive odor to your phone.

When Walleye fishing or Musky fishing and you don't know what you are doing, just tell everyone you are going fishing and be proud of your Pike.

If you are a competitive bass fisherman with a proud history betting a dollar on the 1st, the biggest, and the most, make sure your new fishing buddy knows that the bet pertains to Bass only. Otherwise, you could find yourself in the unique position of paying $3 for the 2-inch brim your friend catches on a slow bass day. There is nothing you can do until you go fishing again to forego the smack your friend will give you about beating you 1 brim to ZERO. Smile and take it like a man.

If your best friend had the foresight to tie a worming hook on his line the night before, attach a Marlboro Red to the hook when he is not looking. He will have to change his hook because fish hate nicotine. I call this tip "The Great Equalizer".

If you are using aluminum stringers while fishing on a power boat with 25 horses or more in the engine, write a note on the back of your left hand to remind you to pull the stringer in when you move to another spot. There is a nice stringer of Pike at the bottom of Leech Lake, MN.

If you use corn to fish for trout like many do in the South, only buy the can you are going to fish with that day. Don't buy the potato and a can of corn to go with your fish dinner until you are on your way home with fish. You can jinx the whole day by assuming you are eating fresh trout for dinner.

While bank fishing and working your way around a damp cove, use a stick to check the ground before your next step. Remember that sinking slowly is still sinking.

If you are straight-line cat fishing on the bottom and using pole holders in the ground, you can catch finicky catfish by getting your feet tangled up in your buddy's line. Put on leather gloves before trying this. A 3 lb catfish on the line will cut your fingers to shreds when you have to bring it in without the help of a pole or your fishing buddy.

Don't leave the lid cracked on any bait holder temporarily housing any crawling bait. This is especially true when storing it in your wife's car overnight.

(Side-tip) Dried out spring lizards and crawfish on the floorboard of your wife's car look like little Raptors to her. She may end up using your truck until you delouse her car from top to bottom.

When the action is great and you have found the color worm the bass are biting on your Texas rig, you can find yourself running out of that color worm quickly. Turn the worms around and hook them from the tail end. You can also hook the worms "wacky worm" style and fish them the same way. I have caught 6 bass on one worm, hooked all three ways.

Re-sheath your fixed-blade fishing knife every time you use it, and never leave your knife unsheathed, blade up. Bleeding a little is a part of fishing, but stupidity increases the pain and blood flow.

It does seem like a great idea at the time, but don't rock the fishing boat when your friend is taking the first pee of the day off the bow of the boat. He will pee all over your boat or his, neither is good. Furthermore you will be looking over your shoulder the rest of the day. Payback is a coming.

Take an uncooked hotdog in a bun with you when you take a kid bass fishing. Put is in a zip lock bag and you will have bait for brim and perch fishing when the bass fishing slows down mid-day. Kids are happy catching any fish at all, so pick up the activity a little and switch to perch fishing. Remember that you can either "take a kid fishing or go fishing". It is very difficult to enjoy doing both, so put a smile on a kid's face and catch some fish.

Chapter VI

Life or Death on Leech Lake, MN

Life or Death on Leech Lake, MN

While fishing Leech Lake alone, I almost qualified for the Darwin Awards. You know the website dedicated to those who through unnatural selection take themselves out of the gene pool with stupid mistakes and missteps. Leech Lake is the 3rd largest lake in Minnesota. It is owned by the Chippewa Indians and has limited structure surrounding the lake. At night, it can look like a dark ocean above an endless sea of walleye, pike, and muskie. When the wind blows 20-30 mph the breakers can reach 3-4 feet and small fishing boats can get knocked around and over in a split second. It is here that Dale Peterson saved my life, and I learned several valuable lessons. I will never look at Leech Lake the same again.

Dale worked at Anderson Lodge in Walker, MN. All of the Anderson Lodges are huge, clean, warm and perfectly designed for fishing groups of 5-20. Warren runs Anderson's Northland lodge and he has always taken great care of us. Dale was First Mate at Northland Lodge and the best we have ever known. He always kept the boats clean and gassed up. Dale was always around to insure we had everything we could possibly need. Our fish are cleaned before we know it and he always has time to teach us a thing or two. When it comes to tackle though, we go to Reeds Family Outdoor Fitters, one of the greatest hunting and tackle stores on the planet. They always have plenty of expert advice on hand, so we always wait to get our supplies there each year. Sure enough the fish are always hitting something new and improved and we usually prove them right. On multiple occasions a member of Reeds staff has dropped everything to assist me for 20-30 minutes. I don't know the first thing about catching walleye, pike or the mythical musky. I say "mythical" because in ten years our fishing parties of 10-15 big, bad, and bold anglers have yet to boat a musky. None of us can cast monster baits worth a flip, but there ought to be at least one of these elusive creatures in a kamikaze feeding frenzy when we pass trolling.

My brother-in-law Martin runs the show every year and about 10-15 brothers, friends and in-laws head to Walker, MN for a long fishing weekend. The rush is on the meet up at Charlie's ASAP. We will be there until Charlie's closes the first night, but we are always in a rush to get to our favorite bar. Everyone in town is usually getting ready for the Ethic Fest. The "Ethnic Fest" is a "Celebration of Cultural Diversity" and the city of Walker becomes one of the friendliest places on the planet. The festival begins for us with the first pitchers of beer and shooters on Wednesday night, but the celebration is always on Saturday.

This was my first year on the trip and I had heard of an initiation. I knew I needed to "man-up" and pick a drink. Once I had picked a shooter, I knew that 10 more were right behind it. It was the responsibility of all attendees to buy at least one shooter for all rookies. I picked Kamikazes for the vodka content. I knew I could hold my vodka. In a vein attempt to try and keep a long story short, like an idiot, I drank everything that came my way and even bought a few of my own. A side note needs to be mentioned here. I won a dart game after 24 shots of Kamikazes against Brian at Charlie's at 1 AM. I could not see a clear dartboard, but one does not have to see the dart board when competing with any of my brothers. Brian is one of my 5 brother-in-laws, but they are all like brothers to me. We will compete and bet on anything that can be observed, caught, thrown, or spewed over the entire weekend. The night ends with me holding my liquor, which was my next big mistake.

I should have purged my system with my finger or another shot. Yes, one more shooter would have done the trick.

The next morning there were white caps as far as the eye could see, but everyone was ready to brave the lake anyway. The plan was to cross the main lake and get to Boy Bay. We knew it would be calm there, but it was 5 miles of ruff riding. As hard as I tried, I just would not be able to go until I had taken some Dramamine. The guys left a boat for me and I was to meet them over there, if I felt better.

At this time I was already suffering from alcohol poisoning and the Dramamine was causing rapid and sever dehydration, but I felt better and didn't know my condition. All I needed to do was motor across to Boy Bay and I thought I would be fine. So I loaded up, and covered up in my waterproofing and set out for Boy Bay at 3000 rpm's. I was making decent time over the white caps as I had the wind at my back. I got to Pelican Island and the lake really started getting rough, but the wind was still at my back and I knew it was just a couple more miles.

All of a sudden things started going very wrong. I was alone and a long way from help. The waves began crashing against the hull of the boat spraying me with clouds of freezing lake water. I began cramping in both legs and both arms and did not know how severely dehydrated I had become. I was not sick, yet..., but I knew there was something else going on and I knew I needed to turn around. There is nothing quite like turning into 25 mile an hour winds in a 14 foot aluminum fishing boat with a small engine. I slowed to 800 rpm's. That was about all the bow could take slamming against the 3-4 foot waves. The white caps were so intense the lake looked like it had a winter coat of moving ice and Pelican Island was the only land I could see. This is about the time I began to power puke. My Fraternity Brothers would have been very happy to hear that I could have set new world records for texture and distance.

I was loosing the use of my hands and arms, so I had to lock my arms together through the steering wheel. My legs were up under my seat. I could not feel them or move them anymore, but it was my big feet the Lord gave me that kept me secure as my boots were locked together around my seat. I knew I needed help and I knew I was a dead man if I lost consciousness. My hands were now bent at the wrist through the steering wheel holding my course steady and into the wind. But it was nearly impossible to move my arms and wrists. I kept within sight of Pelican Island and headed back the way I came, I hoped.

Remembering my cell phone was in my shirt pocket under my waterproof jacket, I started to try to unlock my hands and arms. It took over 10 minutes for me to get to my phone, but I knew I had the number to Anderson Lodge, if I could just use my fingers. I was pretty sure I was having a stroke. I could not speak and was still chumming the waters every few minutes, but I could not turn my head much anymore. It was the only time in my life that getting sick into the wind was the least of my worries. I prayed for strength, for my wife and kids, I prayed for grip, I prayed for consciousness, and I prayed that someone would be near the phone, if I could get a call out on my cell. The number for Anderson was the last number I had dialed, so it came right up on my phone. I pushed the button and Dale magically answered. That does not happen very much at most lodges after the fishing parties have taken off for the day. It was difficult to speak, but he got the point. I said, "Help, having stroke, call ambulance, heading in from Pelican, need help!!!"

Dale took care of everything as usual. He called the ambulance and got some help of another to drive and started heading my way in another boat. By locking my arms back in the steering wheel, I was able to keep the boat into the wind most of the time. It was the combination of strong gusts of wind and perfectly timed 4 foot waves that slapped me around like compass in a magnate factory. That steering wheel kept me from flying out of the boat at least 3 times before Dale arrived. I just tried to get back into the wind and stay conscious. I remember Dale kneeling on the bow of the rescue boat coming right at me. I could not go faster than 900 rpm's and I was frozen into position. The steering wheel woke me up 3-4 times by slamming against my forehead as my head bobbed. Dale kept shouting and kept me awake as well, but he was not as effective as the steering wheel.

When Dale reached me, he could not jump onto my boat. We were heading into the wind, bouncing like hell, and I could not unlock my arms to slow my boat. Although he stayed ready to jump and in a prone position the entire way back to the dock, the seas were just too rough. He was my wingman and without him guiding me in, I would never had made it. Dale saved my life that day. The ambulance was there when we docked. It took 4-5 people to pry me up from the seat and get me on a stretcher. It took another hour to get to a hospital and another hour to get a needle in any vein. I survived sever alcohol poisoning, sever dehydration, and Leech Lake at its worst.

It is a glorious thing to be given the gift of life when you know that your own stupidity should have ended it. Our group has learned its lesson. We don't initiate or fish alone anymore. We all have grown to respect the 3rd largest lake in MN, but now it is far more than just a huge lake to me. Leech Lake and Mother Nature taught me some valuable lessons that day. The most important lesson was to respect Leech Lake at all times and it may allow you to live and fish another day.

Chapter VII

Can You Help Me Take
The Hooks Out?

Can You Help Me Take The Hooks Out?

Being a pond fisherman all my life, I have grown to accept losing honey holes every year. Friends and family have had the audacity to move out of subdivisions with incredible bass ponds and lakes without regard to the outdoorsmen in their lives. Thus, I must jump on any newly discovered fishing-hole as much as possible, even if it takes some work. I had heard about an old pond behind some warehouses on land that had been, virtually, uninhabited by humans for at least 10 years. The first time I hiked to this pond I was with one of my fishing buddies. Mike had always been willing to trespass with me a time or two when we were informed of a remote honey hole. After about 800 yards of burrs, chiggers, vines and barbed wire, we finally made it to the pond. As far as we knew it was a myth, but sure enough, there it was. Monet could not have captured the sheer undisturbed beauty. Mike was first to break the glass and throw his "Grass Frog" just off a stump and "WHAM"!!! It sounded like a beaver tail as it snapped his Berkley Trilene 14 lb test. It happened so fast, he could only estimate the fish's weight to be around 30-40 pounds! Well, maybe not, but we knew there was a wall hanger in there laughing at us. We did not catch anything over the next few hours, but we did get the regurgitated "Grass Frog" back in a brief casting contest. Yes, Mr. "Mac Daddy" bass spit that lure back out at us about 3 minutes after he devoured it.

A week later I had the great idea of tackling that pond and getting that wall hanger. I had to hike my way back through the thick brush and briar patches to get to the pond again, but it was going to be worth it. Eventually I made it to the pond and began my first cast with a black Rapala #13; my favorite top-water bait. For those of you unfamiliar with this weapon of choice of many top-water anglers, it is armed with three 3 pronged treble hooks that I have come to know and respect. I was breathing heavy when I arrived, but I was there and that was all that mattered. I had been waiting for this cast my whole life. In a rush, I let out a little too much slack in the line. As I began my casting motion the Rapala #13 brushed a limb behind me and it was thrown off track like an arrow glancing off a leaf. I failed to mention that I was using 2 hands to cast this lure a county mile past the stump holding my bass.

Suddenly, POW!!! I dropped to my knees for over two minutes. I have never been shot, but I thought someone had shot me in the back of the head. I pictured a man in overalls with a shotgun behind me holding a No Trespassing sign. Everything remained quiet and I reached behind my head to feel what might be left after the blast. Embedded in my head, straight up and down, in the middle of my head, was the Rapala #13. Of the six hooks entrenched past their barbs under my skin, none would budge. I tried yanking them out, but just once. The lure and I were now one. I just cut my line and started walking. I looked at the stump and envisioned my bass smiling as I left. As I worked my way back to my car smiling and shaking my head in disbelief, thoughts of my wife's reaction soon entered my mind. I knew she would laugh, but would she be able to pull the lure out and leave my skull in tact? Upon arriving home, I told her "Honey, I caught a big one, but I need you to take the hooks out"!!! She looked at me like I just took a rib off Oprah's dinner plate. As I sat and showed her the damage and explained the situation, she was in no condition to pull out any hooks. We decided that we might need a doctor to stop her from laughing so hard and we may as well get a doctor to remove the hooks in my head, too. So, of course, we went to the emergency room to complete my pubic humiliation.

There must have been a 100 car pile up on GA 400 that day. The emergency room was packed with people broken and bleeding everywhere. I humbly went to the front desk to sign in and began to hear some small snickers and a brief chuckle from the injured and waiting. By the 3rd time I was called up to the nurse's station, everyone had a good chance to view my casting malfunction and nobody, not even the nurses and doctors, could hold back their laughter. In fact the first person to look at my head told me that the doctor would be in to see me in just a minute.

I asked him if he was a nurse and he said "No, one of the nurses knows that I love to fish and she thought I would get a kick out of seeing your head". Two hours later and minus a little hair and a #13 Rapala, I was back at home and resting. My wife was still chuckling from time to time while I rested on the couch, so life was good. I smiled and thought of my bass under that stump. You won today old boy, but I will heal and the laughter will end, someday, and then you will be mine!!!

Chapter VIII

Tips for the Home Front

Always tell your wife you will be home from hunting or fishing 2-3 hours later than you think you will be returning. When you get home a couple hours early, tell her you missed her and decided to come home early. It is all about building up points with her so you can go on your next hunting or fishing trip.

Never leave your camos that are being washed in "No Scent" detergent near the end of the cycle. If you forget to pull the camos out of the wash and hang them outside, your wife or daughter will be sure to add the April Fresh Scent sheets when they put your hunting clothes in the dryer. They can be very thoughtful.

Don't pack your hunting clothes in your wife's suit case. Remember all those shampoos and scented freebies she has taken from all the hotels over the years. If you make this mistake, you will smell very pretty and you may even have other hunters comment on how pretty you smell; which is never a good thing.

Think of dispersing jerky to your friends and neighbors as though every batch is a pay check. Save enough for your wife and kids before they see large bags being given away to everyone else. Wives that love jerky usually don't love your friends enough to give up jerky without a fight!

Save the number of a local florist in your cell phone. Order flowers for your wife if you answered the phone by saying "What?". This will help you enjoy the rest of your hunt and you won't fear going home.

Make sure that your wife and daughter have left to go shopping or are asleep before you string up your neighbors deer on your swing-set out back.

"What!!!" is never a good way to answer the phone during a hunt, no matter when you wife is calling. You will both be pissed and you will get busted by the only deer in the woods later that day while you are sighting in a squirrel or woodpecker.

Never, under any circumstances, describe how quickly and efficiently you gutted your deer or fish when speaking with your wife.

Get ready 2 nights before your hunting and fishing trip so you can take your wife or girlfriend out on a date the night before. The first time you try this, you may catch her off guard so play it up a little. You can make it an early night, but you have a better chance of leaving her happy with a little forethought and a nice dinner date.

After cleaning the fish in your wife's kitchen (yes, it is your wife's kitchen and if you don't already know that there is not much hope for you), fry a couple fresh fillets in garlic and butter. Not only is this a quick hot snack, but your family won't complain about the way the kitchen smells.

Did you know the sound of sharpening hunting and fishing knives on a diamond stone is far more effective at scaring off your daughter's would be boy friends than cleaning your shotgun in front of them? No need to wet the stone, a dry stone gets a better reaction.

Make an extra effort to pick up the meat scraps out of the kitchen after de-boning your deer or fish meat in the kitchen sink. Look on the side of cabinets, and on the sides of the counters, as well as on the wall. Any miss step here will have the wife's "Manson Lamps" on you like a Black Widow spider after bad sex.

Find out your wife's favorite venison dish and let her know if you are running low on that cut of meat by the middle of the hunting season. She will be more encouraging than usual as the season progresses.

Don't complain to your wife about her smelling like field of rose bushes when she comes to bed the night before your hunt. That's romance in her mind and you better not mess up this obvious clue. Just get up early and use a scrub brush with no scent soap in the shower. It is also best not to mention the scrub brush to your wife.

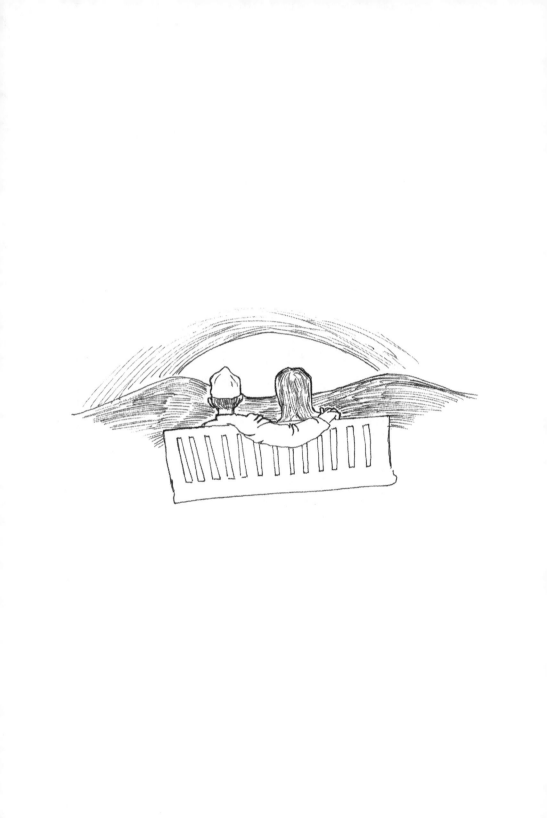

Bring your wife outside and watch the sunset several times during the summer. She will love the romance. As carefully as possible insure she knows the difference between **Twilight** and **Dark**, so she knows when NOT to call while you are hunting and fishing.

Chapter IX

Recipes the Pro's Can't Tell You

Recipes the Pro's Can't Tell You

I'm sure you are asking yourself what I could offer up that Chef Ramsey, Field & Steam, O'Neill Williams and the rest of the great game cooks in the world have not already shared. I have very few to share, but all have caused non-venison eating card carrying PETA members to change their tune a little. I even have clients and vegetarian women asking me when I am going to kill them more jerky?

Kim, my loving wife, belly laughs when I suggest that Chef Ramsey would be hard pressed to best me in a cook off, if I were just limited to Dales Steak Sauce and Worcestershire sauce. She tends to down play my two years of experience as a prep-cook at Chi-Chi's Mexican restaurant. It was there that I unconsciously learned how to use a knife, cutting the fat out of 200 pounds of meat a week. I do most of my own butchering and by the time I am done I am in no mood to make anything from scratch. Less is more unless the smoker is involved or you want a little surf and turf. It is my belief that if you mix two great sauces together you have a new sauce which can be the perfect blend of pre-packaged joy readily available at any grocery store near you. If there is one recipe that is the easiest and most loved by all, it would be my jerky recipe. I share this in hopes that my friends that hunt will start making their own jerky, increasing the local supply as well as my own. I hope that after trying some of these recipes you begin saying to yourself, "Ramsey, bring it on"!

Tim's Famous Jerky

Please be advised! By sharing this jerky with too many people, the demand for your jerky may outweigh your capability of providing enough venison for everyone. I now have to average 4-5 deer a year to have enough jerky to share with friends and have enough for the family. Once the word is out there is no going back. Most of your friends just won't like you for you, it's the jerky they want.

½ bottle of Dales Steak sauce
1/3 bottle of Worcestershire sauce
1 Tbl spoon water (will cut salty taste a little, tweak to your liking)
Add to mixing bowl
Wisk for 5 seconds

Marinate sliced venison for 45 minutes – 1 hour and lay flat on any dehydrator for 12-24 hours. Some pieces will finish before others. Remember to turn jerky once after about 8 hours. It is also good to know that jerky left on the dehydrator over 24 hours can turn into seasoned jerky chips that crumble. Chewy jerky is better than crumbly jerky

For hot jerky I prefer to add 2-3 drops of Dave's Insanity Sauce, but any hot pepper or sauce will do.

Backstraps for Venison Bigots and PETA Card-Carrying Members

If you find yourself cooking for a crowd of skeptics that have never had venison or venison cooked well, knock their socks off with this recipe.

Tenderize venison backstrap with meat tenderizer and a fork or anything that can get the tenderizer into the meat. Some prefer to marinate in Red Wine vinegar over night. This is done by placing the backstrap on a cookie sheet wrapped in plastic wrap and placing it in the fridge overnight. Now just follow these easy steps:

- After tenderizing, unwrap the meat and cut into 1-2 inch small filets
- Wrap each fillet in a ½ inch strip of bacon and place in rows of 5 on a cookie sheet
- After wrapping all filets, use 2 metal kabobs and poke through five filets with each kabob
- Spread apart to allow flame to rise between the filets, if possible
- Marinate each side of the kabobs in Dales Steak Sauce for 30-45 minutes.
- Grill on medium high until cooked medium well with just a touch of pink in the middle
- Take the filets off the kabobs while on the grill and turn the flame up high.

- This will finish cooking the bacon for the next 2-3 minutes
- Serve hot on a platter or serve in a crock pot as finger food at parties

Venison Cheese Dip for the Truly Lazy

The greatest benefit to this dip is that there is just one pan to use and everything is out of your way and is the crock pot 1-3 hours before the guests arrive!!!

1 pound ground venison sausage
2 jars of any cheese dip found in the chip isle of any grocery store
1 jar of any picante sauce found in the chip isle of any grocery store
1 16 oz. bag of shredded Monterey Jack / Colby or Cheddar cheese

- Brown 1 lb. sausage in frying pan well done to absorb most of the grease
- While browning the sausage, pour the contents of the cheese and picante sauce jars into the crock pot along with the entire bag of shredded cheese.
- Pour the hot sausage in with the other ingredients and stir until fully mixed. Cook on high for 1-2 hours before serving stirring frequently.
- Scoops chips work the best if the sausage and picante sauce are chunky

Country Fried Venison or Salisbury Steak

Now we are getting into a little more difficult work, but you may already know that it is worth the effort. For this recipe you will need the following:

4 thawed venison cubed steaks
Black pepper
Garlic Powder
3 eggs
1/3 of a bottle of Dales Steak sauce
Vegetable oil or Olive oil
Flour
1 cup milk
2 cups water

- Scramble 3 eggs in a bowl and set it aside
- Pour 1/3 bottle of Dales Steak sauce into the other bowl and set it aside
- Pour 1 cup of flour on a dinner plate and set it next to the cooking pan that is on the burner you will be using
- Place the bowl with the eggs in it next to the plate of flour
- Place the bowl with the Dale's next to the bowl of scrambled eggs
- Place the meat in a stack on a plate next to the Dales
- Fill cooking pan large enough to hold all 4 cubed steaks with ¼ inch of oil. Test oil by dropping some flour into the oil when you are ready.
- Pepper each cubed steak and powder with garlic to your liking, but don't salt

- Submerge cubed steaks one at a time in the Dale's quickly, then the eggs, then the flour and place in the hot oil
- If cooking Country Fried Steak, cook for 3-5 minutes on each side until golden brown and serve over a bed of rice. Gravy recipe will be below, following the Salisbury Steak steps
- If you are a Salisbury Steak fan, you will only need to cook the steaks for 2 minutes on each side and stack all 4 in a crock pot
- Add 3-4 cups of the gravy below and serve on a bed of rice

For terrific gravy, just put a heaping tablespoon of flour in a cup of milk and use a wisk to blend the flour and milk well. Pour the milk, flour and 2 cups of water in the cooking pan with the used oil. Add a dash or 2 of garlic and some salt and stir with leftover oil and grease. Pour into crock pot right away and cook for 3-5 hours on high. If using the gravy in a side dish, you will have to stir the gravy for about 10 minutes to thicken.

Twice-cooked Venison Hash Brown's

Hash Brown's enough for 4 patties
1 lb ground version sausage
1 lb shredded cheese
Sliced Jalapeño peppers

- Set the oven at 350 degrees
- Cook 4 hash brown patties as usual
- Place all 4 patties on 1 cookie sheet
- Brown venison sausage and insure there are no large clumps of meat
- Put a thin but full layer of sausage over the top of each hash brown patty
- Cover with a mound of cheese and place sliced jalapeños at 3, 6, 9, and 12 like a clock on each mound of cheese
- Heat in the oven for 6-8 minutes or until cheese begins to bubble and turn brown
- Cut each into 4's with a pizza cutter to make this batch server up to 16 small servings for pot luck dinners and such
- No need to cut most, just serve the entire patty right out of the oven and it will be devoured

Sausage Venison Nachos

This dish is similar to the Hash Brown recipe and is the perfect start to any Mexican dinner for 6-8 people. The Chi Chi's way is the best way to make nachos, but the venison adds a great, lean twist. Here is what you will need:

2 lbs venison sausage
12 Toastada shells
2 lbs Monterey Jack & Colby Cheese
Sliced Jalapeño peppers

- Heat the oven to 350 degrees
- Place 4-6 toastadas on 1 cookie sheet
- Brown venison sausage and insure there are no large clumps of meat.
- While browning the meat you can use any Mexican food seasoning packets or try adding just a few tablespoons of Dales with a touch of Habanera pepper
- Put a thin but full layer of fully drained sausage over the top of each toastada (it is very important to squeeze the majority of grease out of each spoonful of sausage in this step before covering the toastada)
- Cover with a mound of cheese and place sliced jalapeños at 3, 6, 9, and 12 like a clock on each mound of cheese
- Heat in the oven for 6-8 minutes or until cheese begins to bubble and turn brown
- Cut each toastada into 4's with a pizza cutter for easy serving and remove all servings from the cookie sheet ASAP and serve hot

Mesquite or Hickory Smoked Venison
(It changes a little each time so this recipe goes nameless)

This recipe is for those who find preparing a great piece of meat a labor of love. Please be advised that when your guests eat this roast, most will roll their eyes back in their head. You did not do anything wrong. They are in a brief state of oral elation much like Jaws snaking on Robert Shaw. For this masterpiece you will require the following:

A smoker, an electric smoker if you want to serve in 4 hours
1 or 2 two lbs venison roasts or backstraps (Load up the rack to the max)
Virgin or Extra Virgin olive oil (still not sure what is meant by Extra Virgin?)
1 Bottle of Dale's
8 oz. Red Wine vinegar
Powdered meat tenderizer (unless you are a purist, then please forgive my mentioning)
Any rub will do (if you are local to Cumming, GA try Wilkes Homemade Marinade)

- Thaw meat and cut off all excess fat
- Tenderize the meat
- Rub the meat with any rub of your choice and place on a cookie sheet
- Marinate in 8 oz of Red Wine vinegar

- Wrap tightly in plastic wrap and place in the fridge overnight
- The next day drain off the remaining Red Wine vinegar
- Cover in Dale's or a 2-1 Dale's to Worcestershire mix
- Re-wrap in plastic and put back in the fridge for 4-8 hours
- Place on the smoker and baste both sides with olive oil
- Re-baste the meat with olive oil every hour
- Serve when there is just a little pink left in the middle (medium well)
- Slice with electric carving knife and serve with dinner rolls at parties

Change this recipe slightly each time and make something unique for you and your guests.

Shrimp Draped with Salmon and Wrapped in Bacon
(I am not worthy of naming this one, I just add the Dale's to make it better)

Now that you have the roasts on and you are all jacked up to cook for the next few hours, this is a great time-filler recipe for the perfect complement. Here is what you will need:

20-30 Jumbo Shrimp (Too big is not a problem here)
1 salmon filet
1 pack of thinly sliced bacon
½ bottle of Dale's Steak sauce
8 metal kabobs

- De-vein, peel, but leave the tail on all the shrimp
- Cut thin slices of salmon at a 45 degree angle in order to fully cover each shrimp
- Lay the bacon out unwrapped and cut the entire slab down the middle
- Blanket the shrimp in the salmon from the top of the back down to about the tail
- Wrap the salmon and the shrimp in a stretched ½ strip of bacon leaving the tail exposed
- Place in rows of 5 or 6 on a cookie sheet
- Skewer 2 kabobs through 5-6 of the shrimp and marinate in Dales on each side for 1-2 hours.
- While the shrimp are marinating wrap the cookie sheet in

plastic and place it back in the fridge

- Remove shrimp from fridge about 15 minutes before mealtime and place on the grill for 3-4 minutes on each side
- Remove the shrimp from the kabobs on the grill and turn up the flame to finish off the bacon all the way around, but don't over cook, just even-out the grilled look of the shrimp

Smoked Barbequed Venison Sandwiches
(This recipe will make the toughest roast melt like butter)

There are several types of roast that we know will be tougher than others. Neck roast and London Broils are two that come to mind. I have found this recipe to be a perfect alternative for this type of meat and you can store it in the freezer for months at a time. To begin with this will require the same steps as you followed in smoking a roast. But immediately after you put the roast on the smoker, you will need the following:

16 oz Apple Cider vinegar
24 oz canned tomato juice
3 Tbl spoons brown sugar
3 cloves fresh garlic finely minced
1 spaghetti bowling pot
1 crock pot
A little Habanera pepper is a good addition if you know your audience

- Add all the ingredients above to the large spaghetti pot and bring to a boil
- Put the fan on high and open the windows and doors, if possible, or you will be overcome by a vinegar tear gas bomb in the kitchen
- Reduce heat and let simmer for 1-2 hours while stirring frequently

- Now is the time to adjust the taste to your liking with more sugar, tomato sauce or other ingredients
- Remember that if you used Dales Steak sauce, don't add too much salt, if any at all
- Pour contents into crock pot and turn on high (you can close the windows and doors at this time)
- The roast should be ready after only about 3-4 hours on an electric smoker
- Remove the roast and either cool and pull the meat or just slice and checkerboard cut the roast
- Mix the sliced roast in crock pot and cook on high for 4-6 hours stirring frequently
- The meat will begin breaking apart and is ready when you can chew it with your tongue

This is a great recipe for reheating while tailgating; lunch at the office, or for just storing the freeze or fridge for a quick meal.

Smoked Venison Brunswick Stew

Here is another way to use the smoked roast. It is also a great way to save a dry roast. This is not my recipe, but I have used it to save an over smoked roast. Change your entre a little and this can save the day with another great side dish!!! Here is what you need:

2-3 lbs of Hickory or Mesquite Smoked Venison Roast
1 can yellow creamed corn
1 can white creamed corn
2 cans diced tomatoes
8 oz Ketchup
2 oz Worcestershire Sauce
4 oz vinegar
6 oz minced onions (I like to use a Vidalia onion here)

Pull or cut the finished roast into chunks and add to a large crock pot. Add the other ingredients stir often. Break apart the meat as you go. It is ready when the meat is tender and pulled apart with very few chunks of meat.

Special thanks to Mike Simonds for helping with the tips and for sharing the outdoors with me all these years. Thanks to David Flores for all the help and design tips.

Thanks to some of my hunting and fishing friends:

Joey Abel	Brittany Abel
Mike Simonds	Mike McClain
Steve May	Johnny Hansard
Jack McClain	David Van Winkle
Josh Pruitt	Rusty Pruitt
Andy Short	Sean Rose
Paul Galvin	Brain Hester
Jim Tilghman	Lynn Merritt
Ray Peteriet	Paul Olsen
Cody Girvan	PJ Girvan
Blake Weihrauch	Martin Vogt
Kenny Dunn	Jack Holcomb
Bob Vogt	Greg Vogt
Wayne Howe	Tom Symcox
Todd Vogt	Cory Barr
Michael Zimmerman	Bill Sauntry
Jimmy Epolito	Simon Cordery
Keith Bulla	Ari Susman

Thank you Steve Rose for doing a great job with the illustrations!!!